MW00365158

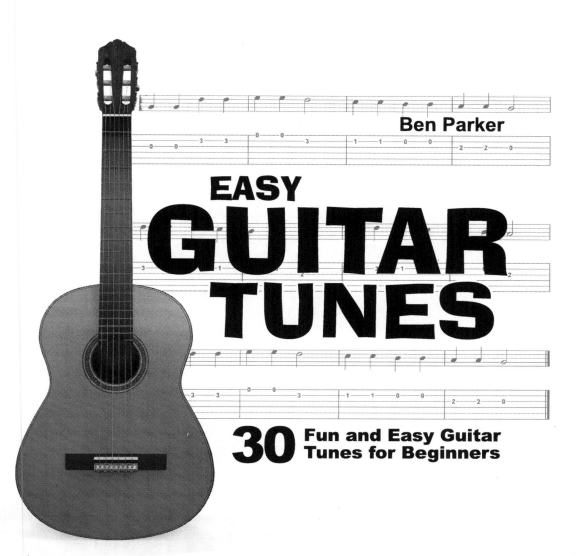

**Ben Parker**

# EASY
# GUITAR
# TUNES

**30** **Fun and Easy Guitar Tunes for Beginners**

Author: Ben Parker

Editor: Alison McNicol

First published in 2014 by Kyle Craig Publishing

This version updated Dec 2014

Text and illustration copyright © 2014 Kyle Craig Publishing

Design and illustration: Julie Anson

Music set by Ben Parker using Sibelius software

ISBN: 978-1-908707-34-5

A CIP record for this book is available from the British Library.

A Kyle Craig Publication

www.kyle-craig.com

# Contents

# Humpty Dumpty

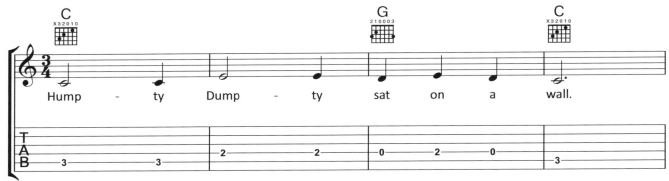

Hump - ty Dump - ty sat on a wall.

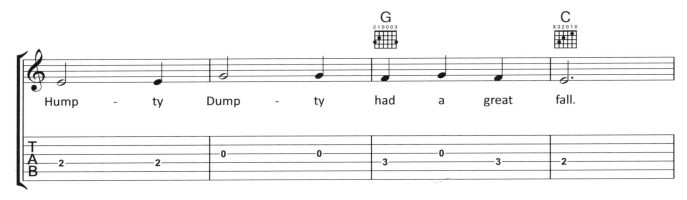

Hump - ty Dump - ty had a great fall.

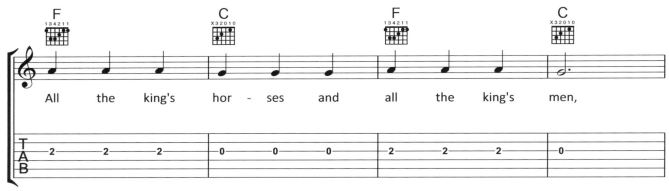

All the king's hor - ses and all the king's men,

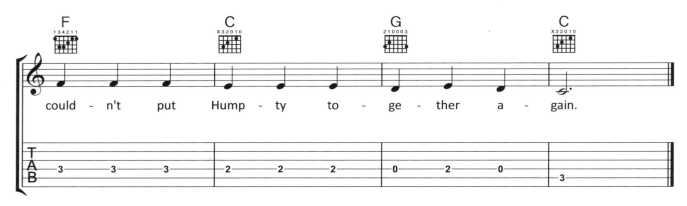

could - n't put Hump - ty to - ge - ther a - gain.

# Oh When The Saints

Oh when the saints,_____ oh when the saints,_____ oh when the

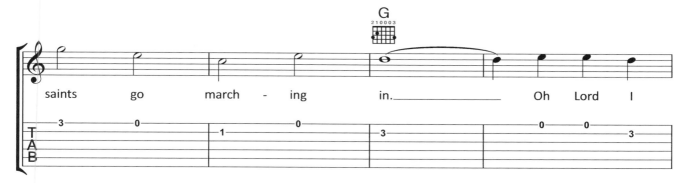

saints go march - ing in._____ Oh Lord I

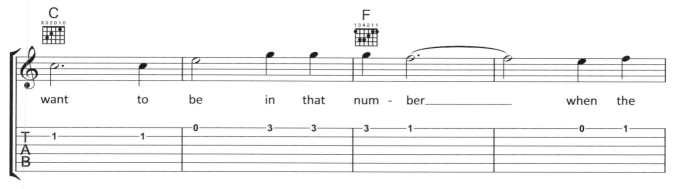

want to be in that num - ber_____ when the

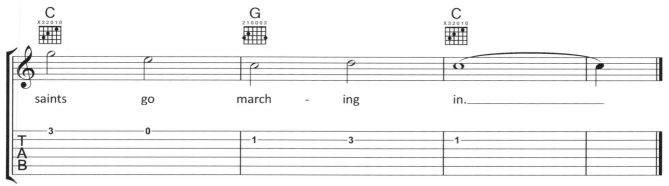

saints go march - ing in._____

5

# The Grand Old Duke Of York

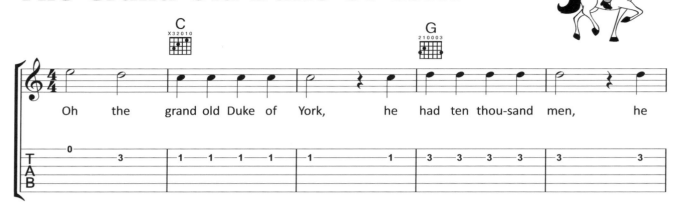

Oh the grand old Duke of York, he had ten thou-sand men, he

marched them up to the top of the hill and he marched them down a - gain.

# Skip To My Lou

Skip, skip, skip to my Lou. Skip, skip, skip to my Lou.

Skip, skip, skip to my Lou. Skip to my Lou, my dar - ling.

# Scarborough Fair

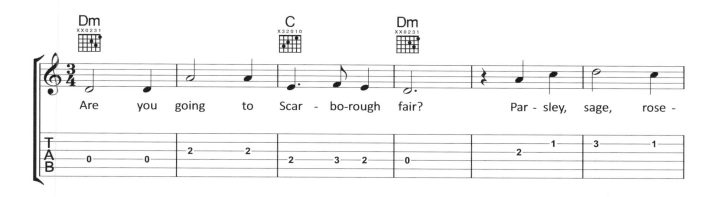

Are you going to Scar - bo-rough fair? Par - sley, sage, rose -

ma - ry and thyme. Re - mem - ber me to one who lives

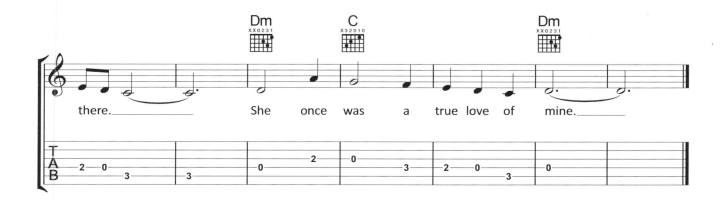

there._____ She once was a true love of mine._____

# My Old Man

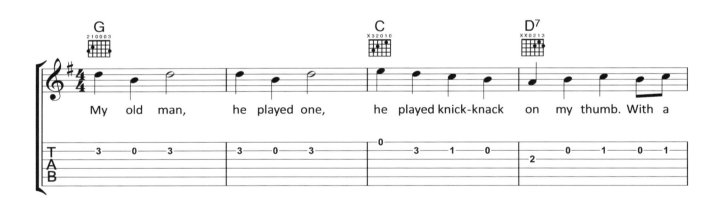

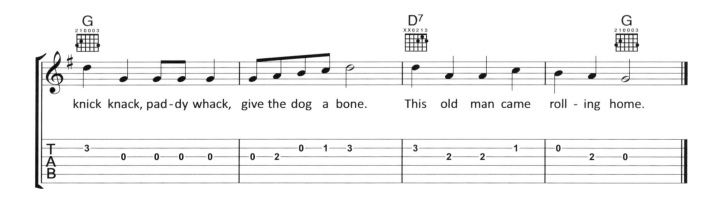

# Scotland The Brave

Hark, when the night is fall - ing, hear, hear the pipes are call - ing

loud - ly and proud - ly call - ing down through the glen. There, where the hills are sleep - ing

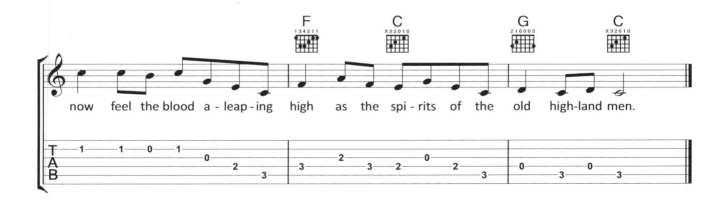

now feel the blood a - leap - ing high as the spi - rits of the old high-land men.

# Home On The Range

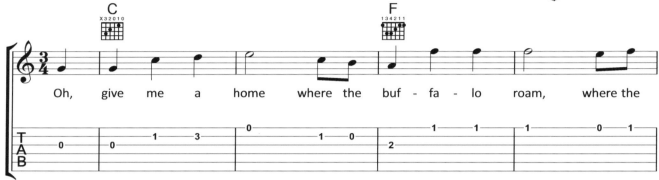

Oh, give me a home where the buf - fa - lo roam, where the

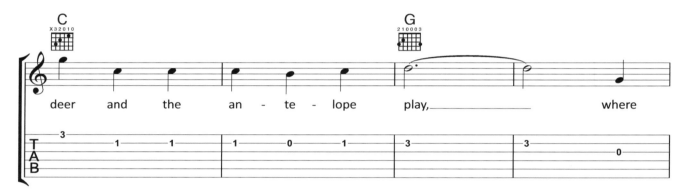

deer and the an - te - lope play, _____ where

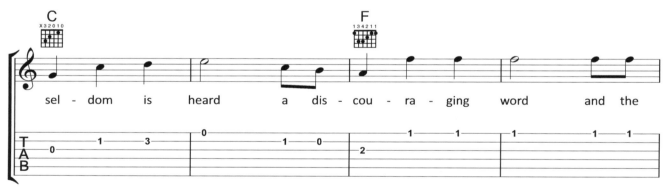

sel - dom is heard a dis - cou - ra - ging word and the

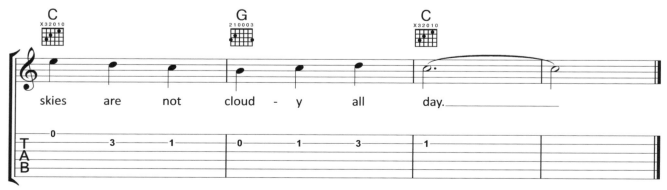

skies are not cloud - y all day. _____

# Old MacDonald

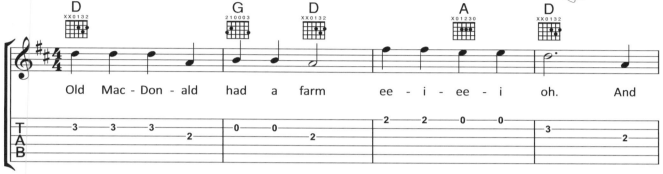

Old Mac-Don-ald had a farm ee - i - ee - i oh. And

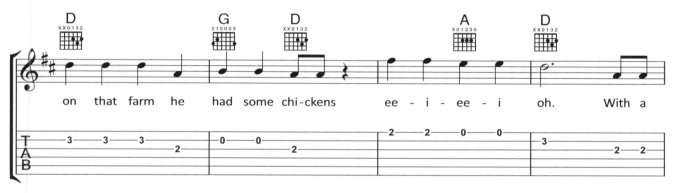

on that farm he had some chi-ckens ee - i - ee - i oh. With a

cluck cluck here and a cluck cluck there, here a cluck, there a cluck,

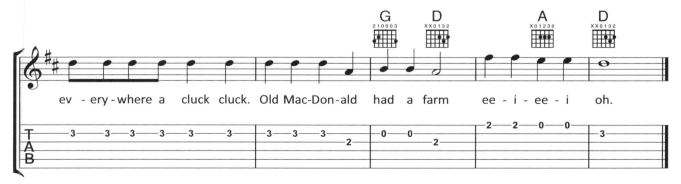

ev - ery-where a cluck cluck. Old Mac-Don-ald had a farm ee - i - ee - i oh.

# Comin' Round The Mountain

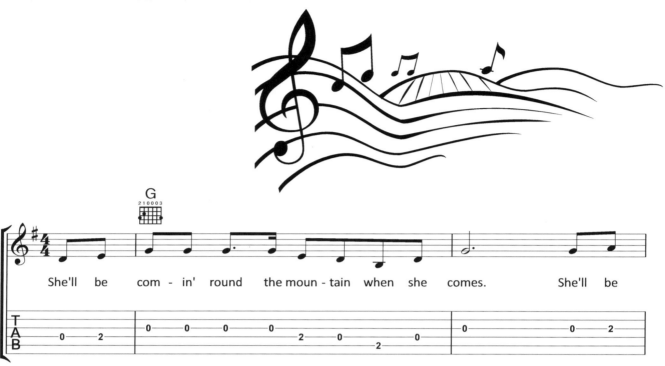

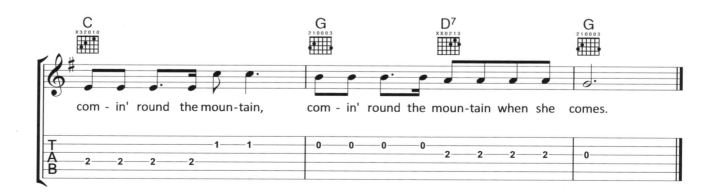

# Hush Little Baby

# Clementine

# All Things Bright And Beautiful

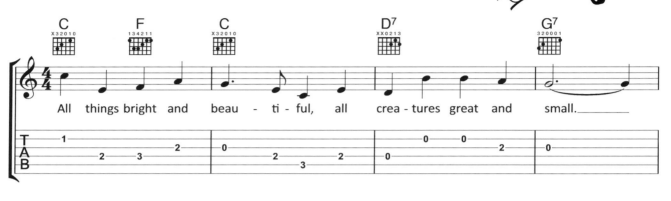

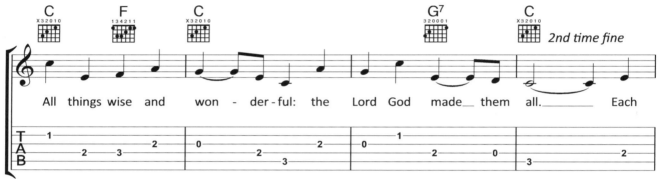

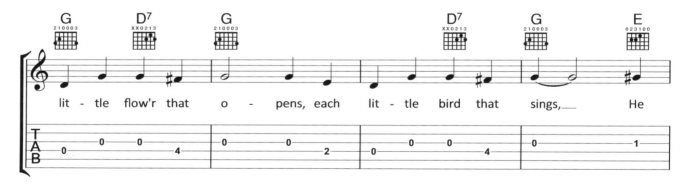

# Song Of The Volga Boatmen

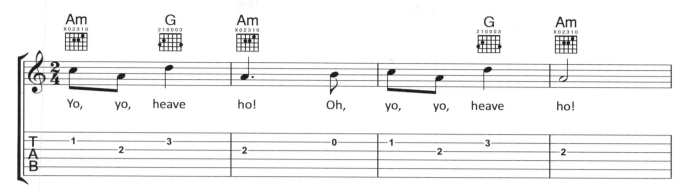

Yo, yo, heave ho! Oh, yo, yo, heave ho!

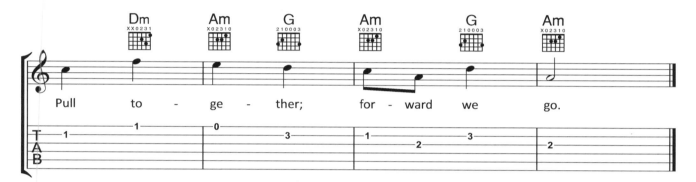

Pull to - ge - ther; for - ward we go.

# Dear Liza

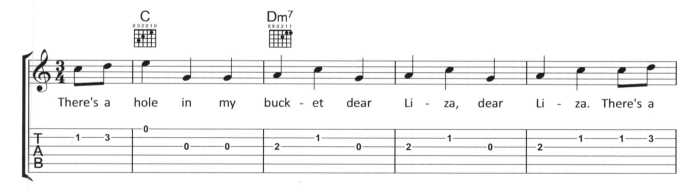

There's a hole in my buck - et dear Li - za, dear Li - za. There's a

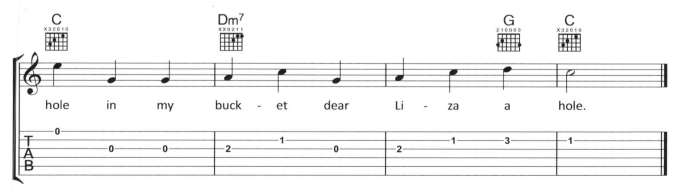

hole in my buck - et dear Li - za a hole.

# Amazing Grace

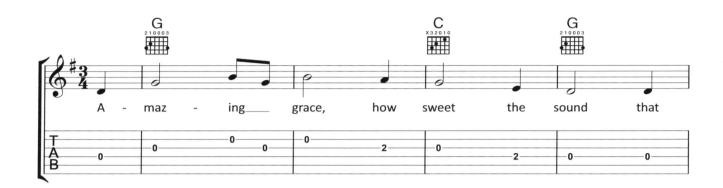

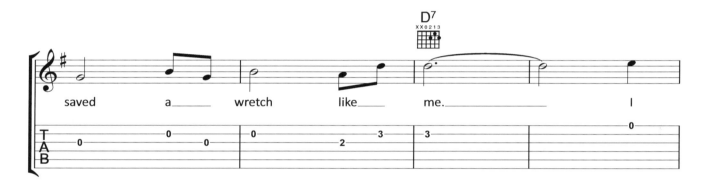

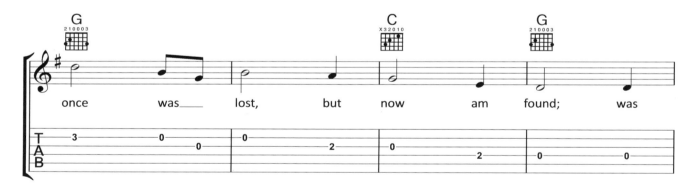

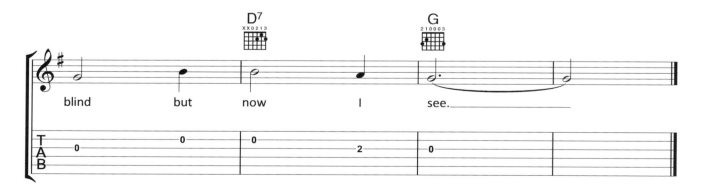

# My Bonnie

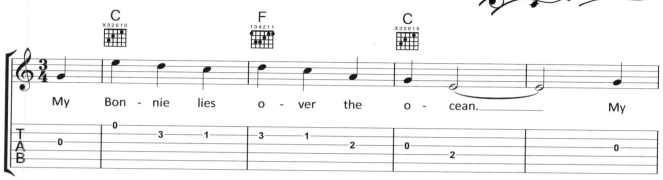

My Bon - nie lies o - ver the o - cean._____ My

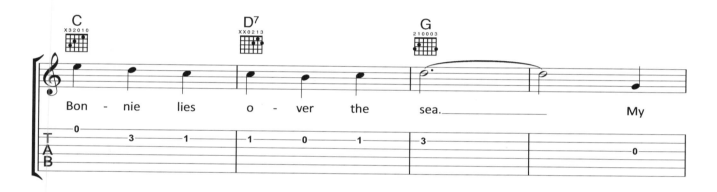

Bon - nie lies o - ver the sea._____ My

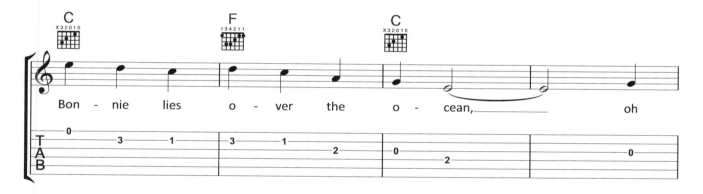

Bon - nie lies o - ver the o - cean,_____ oh

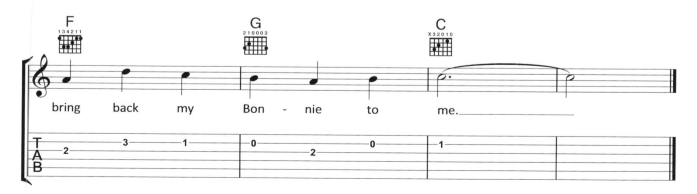

bring back my Bon - nie to me._____

# I Saw Three Ships

# Au Clare De La Lune

# Swing Low, Sweet Chariot

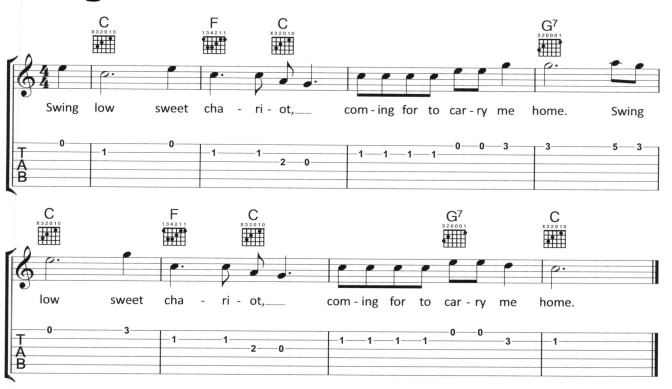

Swing low sweet cha - ri - ot,___ com-ing for to car-ry me home. Swing

low sweet cha - ri - ot,___ com-ing for to car-ry me home.

# Kumbaya

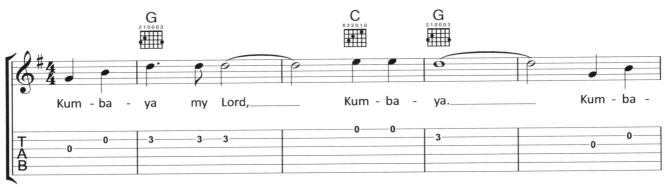

Kum - ba - ya my Lord,_____ Kum - ba - ya._____ Kum - ba -

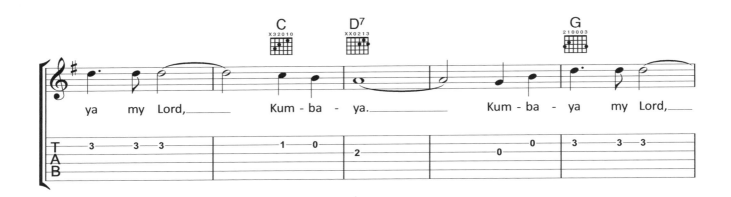

ya my Lord,_____ Kum - ba - ya._____ Kum - ba - ya my Lord,_____

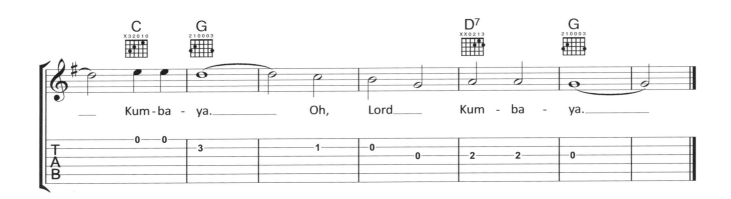

_____ Kum - ba - ya._____ Oh, Lord____ Kum - ba - ya.

# Streets Of Laredo

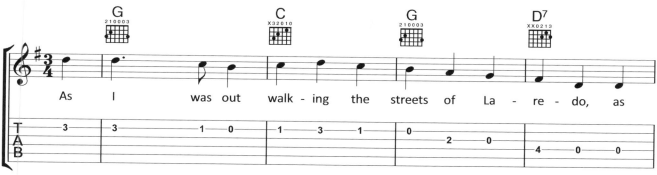

As I was out walk - ing the streets of La - re - do, as

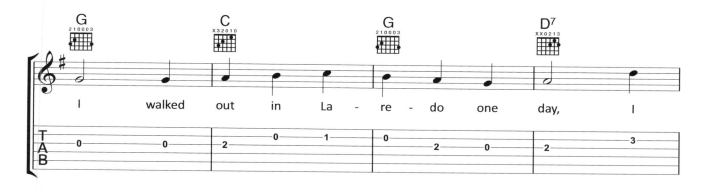

I walked out in La - re - do one day, I

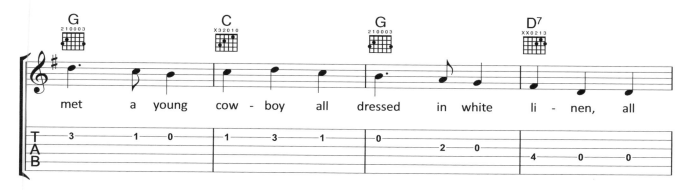

met a young cow - boy all dressed in white li - nen, all

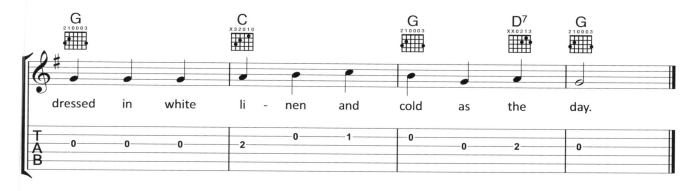

dressed in white li - nen and cold as the day.

# Silent Night

# Oh, Susanna

# Ode To Joy

# Drink To Me Only

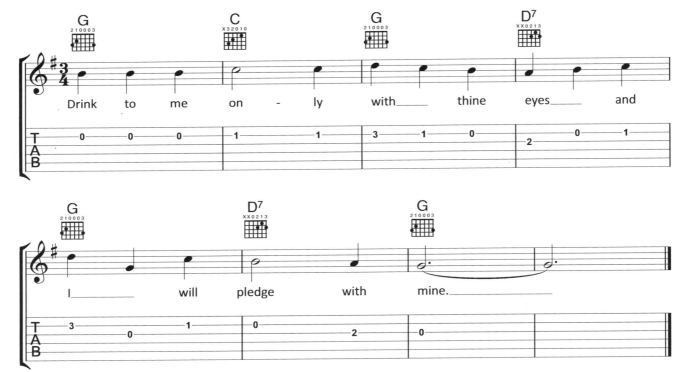

# We Wish You A Merry Christmas

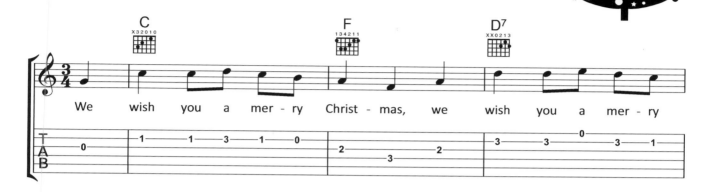

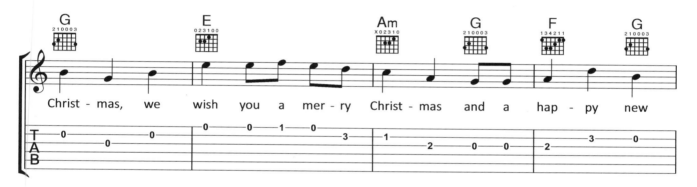

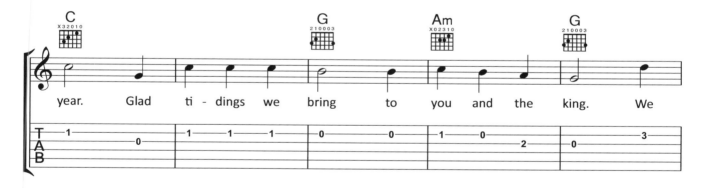

# Oh Little Town Of Bethlehem

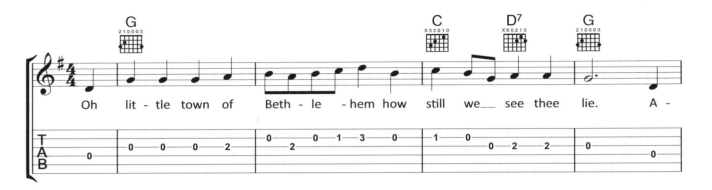

Oh lit - tle town of Beth - le -hem how still we__ see thee lie. A -

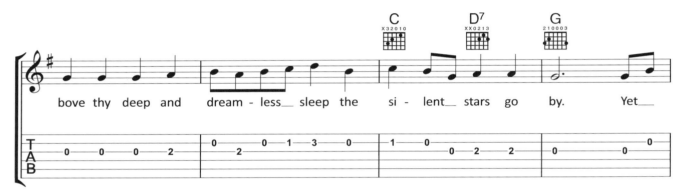

bove thy deep and dream - less__ sleep the si - lent__ stars go by. Yet__

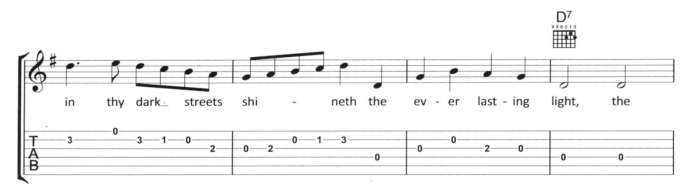

in thy dark. streets shi - neth the ev - er last - ing light, the

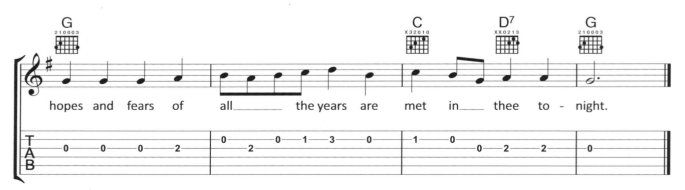

hopes and fears of all_____ the years are met in__ thee to - night.

# Good King Wenceslas

Good King Wen - ces - las looked out on the feast of Ste - phen,

when the snow lay round a - bout, deep and crisp and e - ven.

Bright - ly shone the moon that night, though the frost was cru - el.

when a poor man came in sight, gath-ering win - ter fu - - el.

# We Three Kings Of Orient Are

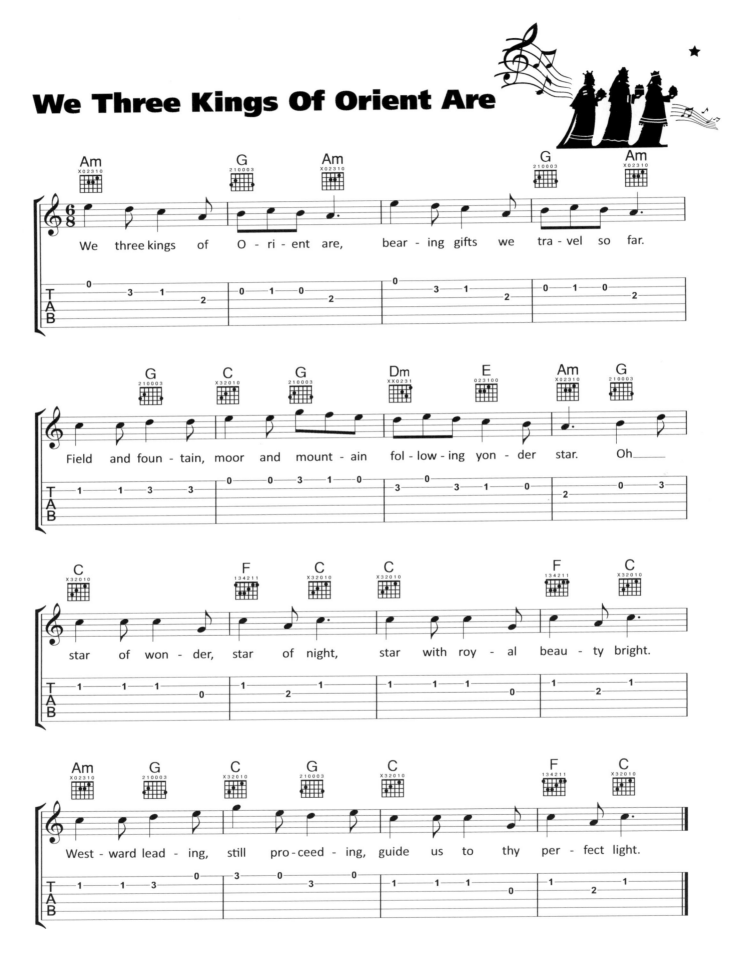

# MORE GREAT MUSIC BOOKS FROM KYLE CRAIG!

**How To Play UKULELE —** A Complete Guide for Absolute Beginners

**978-1-908-707-08-6**

**My First UKULELE —** Learn to Play: Kids

**978-1-908-707-11-6**

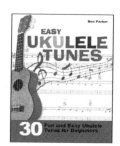

**Easy UKULELE Tunes**

**978-1-908707-37-6**

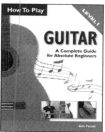

**How To Play GUITAR —** A Complete Guide for Absolute Beginners

**978-1-908-707-09-3**

**My First GUITAR —** Learn to Play: Kids

**978-1-908-707-13-0**

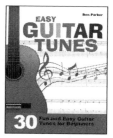

**Easy GUITAR Tunes**

**978-1-908707-34-5**

**How To Play KEYBOARD —** A Complete Guide for Absolute Beginners

**978-1-908-707-14-7**

**My First KEYBOARD —** Learn to Play: Kids

**978-1-908-707-15-4**

**Easy KEYBOARD Tunes**

**978-1-908707-35-2**

**How To Play PIANO —** A Complete Guide for Absolute Beginners

**978-1-908-707-16-1**

**My First PIANO —** Learn to Play: Kids

**978-1-908-707-17-8**

**Easy PIANO Tunes**

**978-1-908707-33-8**

**How To Play HARMONICA —** A Complete Guide for Absolute Beginners

**978-1-908-707-28-4**

**My First RECORDER —** Learn to Play: Kids

**978-1-908-707-18-5**

**Easy RECORDER Tunes**

**978-1-908707-36-9**

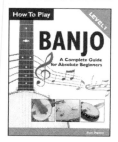

**How To Play BANJO —** A Complete Guide for Absolute Beginners

**978-1-908-707-19-2**

**The GUITAR Chord Dictionary**

**978-1-908707-39-0**

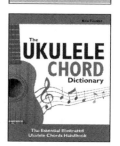

**The UKULELE Chord Dictionary**

**978-1-908707-38-3**

73805320R00018

Made in the USA
Lexington, KY
12 December 2017